SCREWMACHINE/
EYECANDY
OR
HOW I LEARNED
TO STOP
WORRYING

BROADWAY PLAY PUBLISHING INC
56 E 81st St., NY NY 10028-0202
212 772-8334 fax: 212 772-8358
BroadwayPlayPubl.com

SCREWMACHINE/EYECANDY
© Copyright 2007 by CJ Hopkins

First printing: June 2007
I S B N: 0-88145-338-2

Book design: Marie Donovan
Word processing: Microsoft Word
Typographic controls: Ventura Publisher
Typeface: Palatino
Printed and bound in the U S A

ABOUT THE AUTHOR

CJ Hopkins began writing for the stage in 1987, creating
a cut up stage-text entitled ATTIC CLAP THEORY K,
adapted from T S Eliot's THE COCKTAIL PARTY.
In 1994 he was awarded a Drama League of New
York Developing Artist fellowship, and, in 1995,
a development residency at Mabou Mines. The
premiere of his first full-length play, HORSE
COUNTRY, was presented at HERE Arts Center in
New York City in 1997. Since then, Hopkins's plays and
stage texts have been produced regularly in New York,
regionally, and internationally.

Early development of SCREWMACHINE/
EYECANDY, OR: HOW I LEARNED TO STOP
WORRYING AND LOVE BIG BOB was supported
in part by a Developing Artist Fellowship from The
Drama League of New York, and by Monkey Wrench
Theater, which developed and presented a workshop
production of an earlier version of the script, subtitled
VARIATION II, at One Dream Theatre, New York City,
in 1996. Julia Lee Barclay directed the production,
which was performed by Daniel Berkey, Renée
Buciarelli,Vicki Hirsch, Joshua Taylor, Carter Reese,
and CJ Hopkins.

The world premiere of SCREWMACHINE/
EYECANDY, OR: HOW I LEARNED TO STOP
WORRYING AND LOVE BIG BOB was produced
by Scamp Theatre Ltd UK with the assistance of Arts
Council of England, East, and presented at Assembly
Rooms at the 2005 Edinburgh Festival Fringe, where it
was awarded a *Scotsman* Fringe First for innovation and
outstanding new writing. The cast and creative team
were as follows:

BIG BOB .... Dave Calvitto
MAURA BROWN .... Nancy Walsh
DAN BROWN .... Bill Coelius
VERA & CHIP DEVLIN .... Mike McShane

Director .... John Clancy
Stage Manager .... Marianne Davey
Lighting Design .... James Bartrum
Set Design .... Simon Holdsworth
Sound Design .... Damien Coldwell
Costume Design .... Ronnie Dorsey
Fight Director .... Terry King

The New York premiere was produced by Clancy Productions in association with Scamp Theatre Ltd U K, and presented at 59 E 59 Theaters in Spring 2006. The cast and creative team were as follows:

BIG BOB .... Dave Calvitto
MAURA BROWN .... Nancy Walsh
DAN BROWN .... Bill Coelius
VERA & CHIP DEVLIN .... James Cleveland

Director .... John Clancy
Stage Manager .... Chandra Laviolette
Lighting Design .... Lauren Phillips
Set Design .... Simon Holdsworth
Sound Design .... Damien Coldwell
Costume Design .... Ronnie Dorsey
Fight Director .... Terry King

CHARACTERS

BIG BOB, *ostensibly a television game show host*
MAURA BROWN, *a suburban middle American housewife*
DAN BROWN, *a middle American sales representative*
VERA, BOB'*s lovely assistant, a very large man in very*
  bad drag, dress, heels, blond wig, etc
CHIP DEVLIN, *ostensibly the offstage announcer, unseen,*
  but performing live over P A.

SCREWMACHINE/EYECANDY, OR: HOW I
LEARNED TO STOP WORRYING AND LOVE BIG
BOB *is to be presented without an intermission. No late*
seating should be allowed.

ACKNOWLEDGEMENTS

Thanks to Jenny Sutherland, Louise Callow, John
Clancy, Nancy Walsh, Dave Calvitto, Bill Coelius,
Mike McShane, James Cleveland, Marianne Davey,
James Bartrum, Simon Holdsworth, Damien Coldwell,
Ronnie Dorsey, Terry King, Owen O'Leary, Jackie
McGlone, William Burdett-Coutts, Elysabeth Kleinhans,
Peter Tear, Eric Richmond, Jenny Williams, the Scamp
street team, Thom and Robin Schmidt, Billie Jones, Julia
Lee Barclay, Daniel Berkey, Rene Buciarelli, Vicki
Hirsch, Josh Taylor, Carter Reese, Laine Valentino,
David Ferdinand, Dave Overcamp, Ron Gwiazda,
Angele Ayres, Gareth Jeanne, Bowen West Theatre,
De Montfort University, everyone at 59E59 Theaters
and Assembly Rooms, Arts Council England, East to
Edinburgh, and The Drama League of New York.

The fear of tragedy is the fear of permanent
revolution.
Heiner Müller

(An hallucinatory combination T V game show set and suburban American living room. Both aspects represented more or less equally, but not at all realistically. Separate contestant's podiums, for DAN *and* MAURA, *facing out at spectators. A host's podium for* BIG BOB, *downstage, facing spectators.) (Lights up.* DAN *and* MAURA *in position at their podiums. Canned applause punctuates* CHIP DEVLIN's *speech.)*

CHIP: And now, once again, it's time...for The Big Bob Show!

(Game show theme music up full)

CHIP: That's right, it's America's wackiest T V game show...beamed live across the world to over eighty seven countries worldwide! The Big Bob Show, where teams of married contestants pit their wits against each other, go head to head, *mano a mano,* and otherwise fight it out like wild bull roosters, for the chance to win a vast assortment of valuable consumer products! Yes it's The Big Bob Show, the ultimate in viewer entertainment, where we change the rules every week, so you never know what wacky, crazy, unexpected thing will happen next! *(He shifts to fast, businesslike tone.)* The Big Bob Show is brought to you by the L P T Group and its subsidiaries around the world and in the state of Texas. The L P T Group, "We're in the people business!" And by Do-Little, makers of software so simple to use even a little monkey can produce high quality, professional looking reports. Do-Little! "For kids *and* grown-ups." *(Pauses)* And now, hold on to your seats real tight because here he is, your friend and

mine, Mister *money-bags* himself, America's
ambassador of *Culture* ! Big Bob!

(BOB *enters. Canned applause.* DAN *and* MAURA *smile and
applaud.*)

BOB: Hey. Thank you. Thank you. Thank you very
much. Chip Devlin, our announcer, ladies and
gentlemen. Thank you so very much. Welcome back
to the show. Welcome back. Good to have you back.
Good to have you. God, I love this country. What a
country. Thank you. Hey, I don't know about anybody
else out there, but I'm feeling kind of *wacky* tonight.

(*Canned applause*)

CHIP: Just how *wacky* are you feeling, Bob?

BOB: Oh, I'm feeling seriously *wacky* tonight, Chip.
Pretty gosh darned *wacky* I'm telling you right now.
And what it is, I think, is all this *money* in my pocket
here. It's kind of weighing me down! It's making me
kind of *crazy*! It's like I got a ten pound brick here in
my pants, you know, what with all this gosh darned
money in here. That's why I'm just dying to relieve the
pressure and give it all away, if you know what I mean!
So what do you say we get right down to it now and
meet our lucky contestants, Chip.

CHIP: Bob, they're Dan and Maura Brown from
Johnstown, Pennsylvania!

(*Canned applause*)

BOB: Hello Mister and Mrs Brown!

DAN & MAURA: Hi Bob!

BOB: (*Indicating set*) Hey, how about this, folks?
Is this great or what? What a wacky set this week!
The guys really outdid themselves. Kind of a German
Expressionist thing. What do you folks think?

DAN: Yeah! Oh yeah!

MAURA: Oh yes, they certainly did outdo themselves, Bob!

BOB: Looks like some weird version of somebody's *living room* or something. Wow. Weird! Alright. So, what about it then folks? Are you ready to get down to business, and play, uh...whatever it is we're playing tonight?

MAURA: Oh yes we're ready, Bob! We're ready for anything!

BOB: Great. But, more importantly, are you feeling...wacky?!

DAN & MAURA: *(Reciting format-response)* We're feeling *WACKY WACKY WACKY* Bob!

(Canned applause)

BOB: Great! That's just great. Because, let me tell you, *I'm* ready to get wacky, and I mean *totally wacky*. I mean I'm ready to get *BULL GOOSE LOONY* tonight and give away a whole lot of this *FUNNY MONEY*! What do you folks think about that?!

(BOB pulls out a handful of "funny money" banknotes and shakes them in the air. DAN and MAURA applaud. Canned applause)

BOB: Oh yeah! That feels better. Man, I'm telling you. Wow! What a crazy, wacky world, eh? Who could have ever imagined? I tell you, you know, every day I wake up and I say to myself, "Wow!" You know, "Wow!" What a life! Blows your mind sometimes, life. Doesn't it? Yeah. Anyway...welcome to the show, folks, and welcome to lovely *Burbank California*. Long way from home, eh? Where is it again, Johnstown, Pennsylvania?

DAN: It's Johnstown, New York actually, Bob.

BOB: Is it? New York?

MAURA: That's right, Bob. Johnstown, New York.
It's upstate New York.

DAN: There is a Johnstown, Pennsylvania though,
I think.

BOB: Is there? A Johnstown, Pennsylvania. Really?

DAN: I think so, Bob. Isn't there honey?

MAURA: I'm pretty sure.

BOB: Well, imagine that. A Johnstown, New York *and* a
Johnstown, Pennsylvania! A couple of sticklers we got
here, Chip.

(Canned laughter)

DAN: We're from outside of Houston originally, Bob.

BOB: Houston? Terrific!

(Canned applause)

BOB: Houston, *Texas*?

MAURA: That's right Bob.

BOB: The *state* of Texas?! The *lone star* state?!

MAURA: Uh-huh. That's right.

BOB: Wow! Texas! The Alamo! *Fajitas*! Heart of the
country. Wait now, let me picture it...lonely prairie,
little dirt floor shack, chickens, cows, big old dust
storms blowing in from the east...

(Canned laughter)

DAN: Well, no, not exactly, Bob.

BOB: Of course not, Dan. I was just kidding. But tell me
now. I'm curious. How is it, exactly, that a nice couple
like you, a nice couple of contestants from outside of
Houston, ends up all the way up there in Johnstown,
Pennsylvania, or Johnstown, New York, or wherever
it is?

MAURA: You really want to know, Bob?

BOB: *(Pointing out at spectators, as if at a camera)* Why don't you tell the folks at home, Maura.

MAURA: Oh. Well, O K. It's just that, you see...my sister married this guy, whose father—

BOB: So it was like a *family* thing! Great! Wonderful. And what do you do for a living Dan?

DAN: Oh, I'm in sales, Bob.

(Canned applause)

BOB: Sales? Great! What do you sell, Dan? No, wait, let me guess. Commodities, right?

DAN: Commodities?

BOB: No? O K. Not commodities. What is it then? Currency? That's it! Yes! You're a currency trader, aren't you, Dan? Move a bit of that Eurodollar, do you?

(Canned laughter)

DAN: No, no, nothing like *that* ,Bob.

BOB: No? Then what exactly *do* you sell, Dan?

DAN: Uh, gaskets actually, Bob.

BOB: Caskets?! Like for *dead* people?

(Canned laughter)

DAN: No, no. Gas-kets. Gaskets, Bob.

BOB: Gaskets? Gas-kets? What the heck is a Gas-ket, Dan?

(Canned laughter)

DAN: You're kidding again, right?

BOB: *(Winking at DAN, directing his attention towards the imaginary camera)* Just slightly. Yeah. Why don't you tell the folks at *home* what a gasket is, Dan.

DAN: Alright. A gasket...well, Bob, a gasket is like a kind of rubber or plastic seal that—

BOB: And this is your lovely wife...Maura?

(Canned laughter)

DAN: Uh, that's right Bob.

BOB: She certainly is lovely! How the heck are you, Mrs Brown? What a great dress!

(Canned applause)

MAURA: Oh, call me Maura, Bob. We're just plain folks.

BOB: Are you? Sure you are. Of course you are. Aren't we all? Isn't everybody? Listen, Maura, love your hair, but, gosh...I'm almost afraid to ask...I mean, you're not into *gaskets* or anything *weird* or *strange* or *mechanical* like Dan, are you?!

(Canned laughter)

DAN: *(Raises his hand)* Uh, Bob?

MAURA: Oh no. No, Bob. I don't go in for any weirdness, Bob.

BOB: Don't go in for anything *abnormal*, eh?

MAURA: No. Uh-uh. Nothing like that, Bob. We're pretty normal. We're just your average normal regular people, Bob.

BOB: Great. So what are you then, a cleaning lady?

MAURA: What? I don't think I—

(Canned laughter)

BOB: *(Winking at* MAURA, *directing her attention towards the imaginary camera)* Why don't you go ahead and tell the folks at *home* what it is that you do for a living, Maura.

MAURA: Oh. O K. Right. I'm sorry. Well, Bob, I'm a home-maker and a part-time secretary at a corrugated plastics manufacturing company. Consolidated Plastics. We make those panels, those corrugated panels, that go into fences and office dividers and stuff like that. And then on Thursdays I'm treasurer of our local—

(Canned laughter)

BOB: Whoa! Whoa! Too much information Maura! Information overload!

(Canned laughter)

MAURA: I'm sorry, Bob.

BOB: Too many fancy titles for me, Maura. I'll get all *confused* trying to keep track of them all! You don't want to get Big Bob all *confused*, do you?!

(Canned laughter)

MAURA: Well gosh, I didn't mean to—

BOB: Any *kids*, Maura?

MAURA: *(Averts her eyes, whispers down)* No, Bob. No kids.

BOB: No kids?! Not one?!

MAURA: No. We had a son, but, well—

DAN: *(Clears throat)* Could we move on, Bob?

BOB: What? Oh, I'm sorry. I didn't mean to—

DAN: That's alright, Bob. If we could just, you know—

BOB: *(Soft, sincere)* Sure. Sure, Dan. My apologies, folks. I understand. Sorry. Let's just keep rolling. I didn't mean to, you know, get into a *personal* area or anything. *(Switches back to performance mode abruptly)* So, then, how's the *wild, wild West* been treating you? Enjoying yourselves out here in Burbank, California?

DAN: Great. It's just great, Bob.

BOB: Yes, I can tell it is...just by the expression on Maura's face. Tell the truth now, Maura. Are you just a little excited...excited to be here in Burbank, California?

MAURA: Oh yes I sure am, Bob. I've been waiting for this for so, so long!

BOB: I bet it seems like you've been waiting your whole life...like your entire life has been leading up to this.

MAURA: Yes, exactly, exactly, Bob!

BOB: So, just a little excited, are you, to be out here in lovely *Burbank, California*?

MAURA: I'm very, very excited, Bob.

BOB: You're *on* T V...right now, Maura!

MAURA: I know, Bob. It's so exciting!

BOB: Isn't it?!

MAURA: Yes! *(Waves out at imaginary camera)* Hi Cindy!

BOB: Wait, wait, hold on now, Maura. It *is*...or it *isn't*?

DAN: *(Raises his hand)* Uh, excuse me, Bob.

BOB: *(Ignoring* DAN*)* Maura, what are you doing?

MAURA: I'm sorry, Bob. Cindy works with me at the plastics supply. She's in the front office. I told her I'd say something...something on T V—

BOB: That's nice, Maura, but I asked you a question. I said, it *is*...or it *isn't*?

MAURA: I'm sorry, Bob. What is or isn't?

(Canned laughter)

BOB: Exactly! What?! *Is* or *isn't*?

MAURA: What?

DAN: *(Waving)* Bob?

BOB: *(Ignoring* DAN*)* What. Right. I'm asking you, *what*...is so exciting, Maura? Exactly.

MAURA: Oh! Well, this! *This*, Bob. This is. Being here on the show and seeing...well, everything. Gee, I don't know where to start. Everything is! Everything, Bob!

(Canned applause)

BOB: Everything. Everything. *Everything* is so exciting.

(Canned laughter)

DAN: *(Waving his whole body)* Excuse me, Bob?!

BOB: So, Maura, do you have a *real* answer...or you want to pass to Dan?

MAURA: What?

(Canned laughter)

DAN: Bob?!

BOB: What is it, Dan?

DAN: O K, Bob, look. I was just wondering...I was just feeling, you know, uh...wondering when we were going to get *started*. With the *game*, you know?

BOB: Started? Started? We already started, Dan.

(Canned laughter)

BOB: Did you want to go back and start again?

DAN: I don't understand.

BOB: It's a joke, Dan. We're just warming up here. We're just getting to know each other, and all that stuff. We have to find out *who's who*, don't we? So the folks at *home* understand *what's what*...set the *scene* a little, don't we, Dan? A little *background material*...for the folks *at home*? Because, remember, theoretically, they could be right here where you are, right now, one day, playing for the *big money*, on the show, right?

DAN: Right. Sure.

BOB: Or maybe not. Maybe they could never be right here where you are, in which case we don't need to do that at all. But that's up to you to decide! What do you think?

(Standard game show "clock ticking down" sound effect runs.)

MAURA: *(Whispers to DAN)* Oh, I think I see what he's doing now.

BOB: Do you, Maura? That's great! Brilliant! Why don't you go ahead and let Dan in on it then?

MAURA: *(Whispering)* Honey, I think this is one of those times when they don't tell you what the game is, and you're supposed to guess or recognize it from before, from another—

DAN: O K. Right. Guess the Game, or Recognize the Game, or whatever it's called. But what about the rules? He's got to explain. They always explain the new rules of the week. *(To BOB)* Isn't Chip going to explain the new rules, Bob?

(Canned applause)

BOB: *(Hands DAN a few fake bills)* O K! There we go! I thought you'd never ask! The *rules*! Yes! There you go, Dan! Can't play the *game* if you don't know the *rules*! O K, we're almost ready to start now folks, so, let's tell them the rules for this week, Chip Devlin!

CHIP: Well, funny that you mentioned it, Bob, because this week's rules are...

(Brief drum-roll)

CHIP: ...*no rules at all*! It's "anything goes" this week!

BOB: Whoa now, what are you saying, Chip?! *Anything* goes?!

CHIP: That's right, Bob! Absolutely anything! No rules of any kind! Basically, it's every man for himself... who ever ends up with the most *funny money* wins!

(Canned applause)

BOB: Far out! Beautiful! Every man for himself, or *her*self in your case, Maura! Man, I love it...all out total unmitigated *wackiness*! No rules at all. The heck with rules! Whoever has the most *funny money* gets to say *what's what*. Absolutely no underlying system or structure of any kind to rely on. Gee whiz, I guess we'll have to just go ahead and wing it then...shoot from the proverbial hip, won't we? Which, when you think about it, is sort of like *life*, right? You got to just get out there and take your *shot*. "Make it happen!" "Go for it!" Yeah! Wow! Weird! Now then, where were we? Oh yes...I asked you a question, Maura.

MAURA: You did?

BOB: I just said I did. So I must have! Right?

(Canned laughter)

MAURA: I must have, uh, lost track there—

BOB: Or I could be *lying*! But I'm not. Or am I?

MAURA: I'm sorry. I'm a little confused now, Bob.

(Canned laughter)

BOB: Gosh, Maura, I didn't mean to confuse you. Or maybe I did. But seriously, Maura, I just figured, what with all your important positions, that you'd be able to juggle a few *balls*, you know, wear a few *hats*, walk and chew gum.

MAURA: Could you repeat the question, Bob?

BOB: Alright, but just this once. What was the question again, Chip?!

CHIP: Bob, the *question* was, "What, exactly, is so gosh darn exciting, Maura?"

MAURA: Oh! I already answered that, Bob.

BOB: No, you didn't.

MAURA: I believe I did. I'm pretty sure I did. I said everything...being out here, on the show, and all that, and you said—

DAN: I think it's some kind of a trick question honey.

(Canned applause)

BOB: *(Hands DAN money)* Whoa! Look out! Nothing gets by Dan! Sharp as a tack, boy! Analyzing every moment! Better watch out for this one, Maura.

MAURA: *(To DAN)* What should I do?

BOB: Tick tock, Maura!

DAN: Just go along. Answer again.

MAURA: O K, uh...what's so exciting? Well, Bob, the game...

(Canned laughter)

BOB: The game? The game?! That's what's so exciting?

MAURA: Uh...the chance to win things? The chance to win things!

(Canned applause)

BOB: *(Hands MAURA money)* Yes! *Things*! You bet, Maura! So you'd like to win some things?! How'd you like to win a whole wheelbarrow full of things?!

DAN: That's what we're here for, Bob!

BOB: Is it, Dan? That's what it's all about, is it? A wheelbarrow full of things? That's what you're *here* for?

MAURA: We like to have nice things, Bob.

BOB: Of course you do. Who doesn't? Things are great. Pretty little things...like those little porcelain statues... statuettes of poodles and little swan-shaped ashtrays... things like that?

(Canned laughter)

MAURA: Those are nice, Bob. But we like other things too. We like things that are useful too.

BOB: *Useful?* How quaint. Things you can *use.* So exactly what kind of useful things did you have in mind to win tonight, Maura?

DAN: I wouldn't turn down a new power mower, Bob! I'll tell you that. *(Laughs)*

BOB: *Power* mower. Perfect. You can *use* one of those! What about you, Maura? Like a new power mower? Is that what you had in mind, Maura...one of those big ole John Deere *power* mowers, with seats on top, like the Mexicans drive?

MAURA: The Mexicans?

BOB: The Mexicans, who come and do the lawn. Or Guatemalans or whatever they are.

DAN: Well, we kind of do our own lawn, Bob. I do, I mean. But hey, you know, maybe after today...

BOB: Right. That's right, Dan. Maybe after today, if you do really well...in the *game,* I mean...you can quit doing the lawn with your little mower, and hire somebody else to do it *for* you! Doesn't that whole concept just blow your mind?! I mean, what a country, boy, where you can just get up in the morning, and one day, Boom! You're filthy rich! You know what I mean, Dan? Ba-Boom! Jack-Pot! Hey, anything goes, right?! You could wake up rich! You could wake up tomorrow and have a big green lawn just swarming with power mowers and Mexicans and all that. I mean, look at me!

It's possible! Isn't it? You could just suddenly get rich out of nowhere! Like the people in the magazines. For no reason at all.

DAN: Hey, I could certainly live with that, Bob.

BOB: Could you? Could you? Well, there it is. There's the whole thing in a nutshell right there. It's pretty gosh darned simple. What about you, Maura? How would that be? Wake up tomorrow loaded with cash, big green lawn, Mexicans, etcetera. How would that be?

MAURA: Well, that would be great, Bob, but, you know, the thing is, even if we just come out a little ahead, it doesn't really matter, because, you know, it's the winning...it's the winning itself that's so exciting. Even more than what you win.

BOB: (*Hands* MAURA *money*) Yes! There it is! Beautiful, Maura! That's the spirit...the American way! The winning more than what you win! Just to get in there and *win* and *win*. To win the game...regardless of the prize. Could be a half a million dollars. Could be a little plastic whistle. But it doesn't matter. Because the point is the *winning*! Because what else is there, when you boil it right down? I mean, you're either a *winner* or a *loser*, right? You're either *somebody*, and you're rich and powerful, or you're some little *nobody* with an ax to grind. And then you're miserable, and you go around bitching and whining and complaining to anyone who'll listen...usually a bunch of other losers like yourself, and you go around whining about how *unfair* everything is, how the Man is oppressing you, how the poor little working man is getting shafted by the rich all the time...it's like a little *losers club*. But, hey, now, you're not worried about *that*, are you? No! You're not *worried*. You're excited, right? You're excited about winning! Because you feel like a winner! Because you've got that *winning attitude*! And that's what's *really* got you so excited, isn't that right Maura, feeling like a winner?!

MAURA: That, yes, and just being on T V.

BOB: Pretty gosh darn exciting, isn't it, being on *T V*... a *T V* person?!

MAURA: Oh lord yes. I never thought—

BOB: *(Checking his watch)* Kind of the opposite of *boring*, right?

MAURA: Right! U-huh.

BOB: Yeah. So...don't get this excited that often then, eh, Maura?

MAURA: Sure I get excited, but not *this* excited, Bob!

DAN: Uh, Bob?

BOB: *(Pointing out at imaginary cameras)* Look! You're on *T V*, Maura!

MAURA: I know! I know! It's so unreal!

BOB: What's the matter, Dan, don't take her out much?

(Canned laughter)

MAURA: Oh sure he does Bob. We go places. We go all the time.

BOB: I'm talking to Dan now.

MAURA: Oh, I'm sorry.

(Canned laughter)

BOB: That's O K. Dan?

DAN: What Bob? What?

BOB: I asked you a question.

DAN: A question?

BOB: That's right.

DAN: If I take her out?

BOB: Right! Correct. Do-you-take-her-out?

DAN: Wait. Is this for points, Bob?

BOB: Sure, for points, for a lot of points. A hundred points. Just go with me, Dan. Let's get the show rolling here. *(Winking, first at* DAN, *then at spectators)* We're kind of dying here, if you know what I mean, Dan.

DAN: Alright. Alright. I'm sorry, Bob.

BOB: So, then, Dan, do you take her out, or you sit at home, or what, exactly?

DAN: Oh I get it. *(Performing, trying to play along)* Well, hell yes Bob. Sure, I mean, we go out all the time, you know...places.

BOB: Watch your language, Dan. *Family* show.

DAN: Jesus, I'm sorry, Bob.

MAURA: Dan!

DAN: What?

MAURA: You just swore again, honey.

DAN: No I didn't.

MAURA: He got it from his father, that swearing, Bob.

BOB: His *father*? Hmm. A doctor, was he?

MAURA: A minister, actually.

BOB: Unitarian.

MAURA: Oh my God! How did you know?!

BOB: Wild guess. No, actually, I was a psych major, Maura, back in school...had to learn how to *read* people, you know, the *subtext*. But, I'll tell you what...why don't we leave all that for later, seeing as we should probably get things *going* here before our *sponsors* cancel us for bombing.

(Canned laughter)

BOB: So, Dan, take the wife out, do you?

DAN: Sure. Oh yeah.

BOB: Great. Where?

DAN: Where?

BOB: Yeah, where, exactly, do you take her? I mean, this is still *America*, right? There are only about a billion and a half places you could go to be *entertained*, aren't there, Dan?

DAN: Uh. I don't know. We go all kinds of places.

BOB: Great. Name *one*.

DAN: Restaurants.

MAURA: Shopping!

BOB: Shopping! For *things*! Good! Brilliant!

(Canned applause)

DAN: We just went bowling.

(Canned applause)

BOB: Bowling?! Marvelous! America's pastime. Big *bowler*, are you Maura?

MAURA: Well no, not really, Bob.

BOB: She says she doesn't *bowl*, Dan.

DAN: Oh, she bowls.

BOB: Oh I bet she does.

MAURA: Mostly I like to watch, Bob. Sometimes I'll roll a ball or two.

BOB: Roll a couple of *balls* now and then, do you, Maura?

(Canned laughter)

DAN: You do too bowl honey. You bowled the other night.

MAURA: *(Embarrassed)* Well, sure—

DAN: She's just not very good, Bob.

BOB: Sorry to hear it. My sympathies, Dan. *(Clears throat)* So, do you bowl or not, Maura? Let's try to stay with the point here. Boy, I'll tell you, this is fascinating stuff.

MAURA: I do bowl sometimes.

BOB: Great. So you bowl. You admit to *bowling.* You take *the ball* and roll it down *the lane* and the little *pins* fall down?

(Canned laughter)

DAN: Say yes honey.

BOB: No helping Dan.

MAURA: I guess I do, Bob. I bowl...sometimes. But not like every weekend or anything.

BOB: You wouldn't be fibbing to old Bob now, would you, Maura?

MAURA: It's just that I'm so bad at it, Bob.

BOB: Yeah, that's what Dan just said, Maura, how you're not very good at it at all, which is sad. But why do you think that is, Maura? I mean, is it just lack of talent, you think, or is it more that you don't enjoy *handling the ball* all that much? I only ask because, you know, they have books now that you can read and they'll show you all the right positions—

(Canned laughter)

DAN: Uh, Bob?

BOB: Yes, what is it Dan?

DAN: Uh, O K, I know we're just talking here...warming up like you said. I mean, I'm just saying, we've been doing this for like...a *while*. I mean, shouldn't we start *playing*...playing for *real*, get things *going* like you said, Bob?

BOB: What is it, Dan? Somewhere you're supposed to be? Got some important *gasket business* to attend to, do you?

(Canned laughter)

DAN: No. I just—

BOB: *(To DAN, but facing out at spectators)* What are we, *boring* you, Dan? Don't find the conversation *interesting*? Is that it? It's not *engaging* you?

DAN: No, I just thought we were supposed to—

BOB: Hey! Hey! Dan! Who's running this show, you or me?

(Canned laughter)

DAN: I'm sorry. I thought it—

MAURA: You shouldn't interrupt, honey. If you drift off, you know, you just pick up wherever you come back in.

DAN: What are you talking about?

BOB: Gee whiz, Dan. I don't recall seeing *your* name on the credits anywhere. I don't recall that on the big marquee outside, "The Big Bob Show, with little Dan the Gasket Man"!

(Canned laughter)

DAN: I'm sorry. I guess I got a little impatient, Bob.

BOB: You want to come up here and do this, Dan?

DAN: Jesus. I said I was sorry, Bob.

BOB: *(Winking and grinning at* DAN, *as if to encourage him)*
I asked you a question, Dan. Do you want to come up
here and do this?! Is that what you want? To come up
here and *take over*?!

(Canned laughter)

DAN: *(Chuckling conspiratorially, trying to play along)* Oh.
No, Bob. I wouldn't want to do that.

BOB: Be honest, Dan, if you want to come up here,
because this may look easy to you—

DAN: No, no, I'm sorry if I gave you that impression,
Bob. Because I sure wouldn't want to do *that*. If you
know what I mean. *(Winks conspiratorially)*

BOB: *(Drops grin, cold)* No, I *don't* know what you mean,
Dan. Do you know what you mean? Look, Dan, here
I am, just trying to get things rolling, get things set up,
trying to flesh things out in a way that people can
identify with, so we can go ahead with *the game* and all
that...and they can *identify*...with you, or whatever...and
here *you* are, interrupting me every time... Never mind.
Look. Tell me something, Dan. Level with me now.
You're not one of those *subversive* types, are you?

DAN: Subversive? What do you mean, Bob?

BOB: You know, like one of those *terrorist* types that
goes around putting those little *bombs* all over, all those
little booby traps, to sabotage things, to disrupt the
normal flow of life and keep everyone on *edge* and
jumpy all the time?

DAN: A terrorist?! Hell no, Bob! Jesus, are you serious?

MAURA: You're swearing again honey.

BOB: It just seemed like you wanted... like you were
resenting my position here, or questioning my
authority or... Well, I don't know. Maybe I'm
over-reacting a little. So you're sure you're not one of

those saboteurs, Dan, those bitter little Third World *identity crisis* types?

(Canned laughter)

DAN: One of what?

BOB: I'm sorry. Am I going too fast for you, Dan? I said, you're not one of those *topple-the-tower* types, are you...tear down the *castle* or the *skyscraper* or whatever?

DAN: No, Bob. Jesus, I'm a Republican for Christ sakes!

MAURA: Dan!

BOB: Good. That's real good, Dan, *BLASPHEMER*, because I'll tell you, if there's anything that'll kill a show, it's one of those Oedipal transference types coming in here to blow off steam. Bo-ring! Bo-ring! But you're not one of *those*, right?

DAN: No way, Bob!

BOB: Good. Excellent. So how about doing me a favor then, and just keep your mouth shut when I'm talking to Maura? Think you could manage that?

DAN: Wait. What's going on here?

BOB: *(Laughing, puts arm around* DAN*)* Whoa! Take it easy! Just kidding around, *Dad,* uh, *Dan!* Just pulling your chain a little. Lighten up, buddy!

(Canned laughter)

MAURA: *(Laughing)* He got you honey.

CHIP: Remember, anything goes, Dan! Every man for himself!

BOB: That's right, Chip. Every man for himself. But seriously Dan, you're right, you know. I was really beating that bit into the ground, that "getting to know you" bit. I was beating that bit to death, way past where it served any purpose at all. I mean, granted, it's fascinating stuff, you know... where you're from...what you do for a living...what's your favorite color. People. Wow. There are so many levels. I could just explore all day...explore the psychological depths all day, but, well. *(Pulls out Q & A flip card)* Anyway. *(Reading from card)* What's the capitol of Iowa, Dan?

DAN: Capitol of Iowa?

(Canned laughter)

BOB: Capitol of Iowa.

DAN: Oh, O K, these are the questions now. Capitol of Iowa. Uh—

(Canned laughter)

BOB: Right. No capitol of Iowa. *(Takes money back from DAN, takes out another card)* O K. Maura, in what year were inalienable human rights first established?

DAN: Des Moines!

(Canned laughter)

BOB: Too late, Dan. What year, Maura?

MAURA: Forty six, Bob?

(Canned applause)

BOB: *(Hands MAURA money)* Close enough, Maura. Right around the *Holocaust* anyway, right? In any event, you support that, don't you, Maura? Inalienable human rights for everyone, that everyone is *born* with? You're *for* that, aren't you?

MAURA: Human rights? Oh yes, I'm for that. Everybody should have human rights, Bob.

BOB: *(Hands MAURA money)* Even Poles?

MAURA: Huh?

BOB: Poles. *Polish* people. From *Poland*, Maura.

MAURA: Oh yes. Yes! They do have them, don't they?

(Canned applause)

BOB: *(Hands MAURA money)* Sure they do. They're born with them. Everyone is. And no one can ever take them away. What about *black* people? Should they have them?

MAURA: Of course! Yes!

(Canned applause)

BOB: *(Hands MAURA money)* Of course. Of course. What about...homosexuals, Maura?

MAURA: Uh, yes, I guess so, Bob. If everyone is born with them.

(Canned laughter)

MAURA: Well, maybe not.

(Canned laughter)

MAURA: I...I don't know, Bob.

BOB: *You're* not, by any chance...

(Pause)

MAURA: *(Nearly shrieking)* A homosexual?! No Bob!
(Canned laughter)

BOB: Uh-huh. O K. And what if I were to tell you that I...was a homosexual?!

MAURA: *(Panicky)* That would be O K with me, Bob!

(Canned applause)

BOB: Would it? That's great! Then, in that case, Maura, I guess I would be *allowed* to be a homosexual. I mean, as long as it's O K with *you*, that is.

MAURA: Oh God, that's not what I meant, Bob!

(Canned laughter)

BOB: Relax, Maura. I'm not a homosexual.

MAURA: Oh! Whew! You were just—

(Canned applause)

BOB: *(Hands MAURA money)* Having you on, yes. On the other hand, I could just be in the closet, Maura. I could just be out here *acting* normal!

(Canned laughter)

BOB: But then, what difference does it make, right?

MAURA: Right!

BOB: Right. Precisely, Maura. Dan! Cleopatra starred Richard Burton *and...*

DAN: Elizabeth Taylor!

(Canned applause)

BOB: *(Hands DAN money)* There we go, Dan! There's a response. Better now, Dan? Things feeling better... a little more *normal*, like what you're used to? O K, Dan! On a scale from one to ten, how would you rate your *flight* out here?

DAN: I'm sorry?

BOB: Your *flight*, out *here*, for the *show*...the *friendly skies*. On a scale from one to ten. Would you give it a one, or a seven, or what?

DAN: Uh, well, we didn't fly out exactly, Bob.

BOB: You didn't *fly* out? Not exactly? Well how the heck did you get here then?

MAURA: We came out on the bus, actually, Bob.

(Canned laughter)

BOB: The bus? The *bus* bus? Like the *Greyhound* bus?

(Canned laughter)

DAN: *(As BOB takes money from him)* That's right. The bus.

MAURA: Are we still playing now?

BOB: *(Whips out a question card)* Columbus sailed the ocean blue in...

MAURA: Fourteen ninety two!

(Canned applause)

BOB: *(Hands MAURA money)* What is it, Dan, are you scared of *airplanes*? They *remind* you of something... that big old *fuselage* soaring around in the heavens?

(Canned laughter)

DAN: No, that's not...planes are fine, Bob.

MAURA: It's just that we're trying to save money, Bob. We're trying to save up for—

BOB: Wait. Wait now...you couldn't cut loose the money for a *plane ticket*, Dan?!

(Canned laughter)

DAN: Like Maura said, Bob, we're saving up for—

BOB: Gasket sales a bit *off* are they, Dan?

(Canned laughter)

DAN: Yeah, well, things are tough all over.

BOB: Are they? I hadn't noticed, to tell you the truth. So I guess they're not tough *all* over, Dan. Oh, by the way, great *haircut*, Dan. Hell of a *haircut*! *(Turns away, as if suddenly distracted)* Oh, man, what's that *smell*?!

MAURA: Are we still playing, Bob?

BOB: Sure we are, Maura. Dan! On a scale of one to ten, how would you rate your... *(Stifles laughter)* ...bus trip out here?

(Canned laughter)

BOB: *(Waving money at DAN)* Come on, Dan. Be a sport.

DAN: I guess I'd give it a five, Bob.

(Canned applause)

BOB: *(Hands* DAN *money)* A five Good. Brilliant. Maura?

MAURA: I'd give it a five too, Bob.

(Canned applause)

BOB: *(Hands* MAURA *money)* What about the *hotel*?

MAURA: Oh, I'd give the hotel a ten!

(Canned applause)

BOB: *(Hands* MAURA *money)* What about you, Dan?

DAN: I'd give it a ten too, Bob.

(Canned applause)

BOB: *(Hands* DAN *money)* Fancy, huh?

MAURA: Oh God yes! Whoops! I'm sorry. I interrupted.

BOB: Ever stay in such a fancy *hotel*, Dan?

DAN: It's a good hotel. Look. What's the point of—

MAURA: Good? It's better than just good, honey.
It's a wonderful hotel, Bob! The room is...it's bigger...
it's bigger than our house! The bathtub...it's marble,
like real marble, from Italy or somewhere.

BOB: How's the *toilet*, Dan? *Toilet* O K?

DAN: What?

MAURA: You know Bob, normally we just stay at a
Quality or a Motel Six or something. When we're
driving, that is. Or sometimes we camp out, but—

BOB: Wait. You don't mean you sleep *outside*...like a
homeless?!

(Canned laughter)

MAURA: Oh no, not like that, Bob. Not like a homeless.
Like at a campground, you know. We stay at
Campgrounds of America, mostly. Dan loves the
wilderness. They give you this guide. It's like a map
of all the wilderness areas, so—

BOB: Wait a minute, Maura. A *map*...for *wilderness* areas?

DAN: Can we move on *please*?!

BOB: *(Takes money from* DAN *and* MAURA*)* Gosh, I don't
know, sleeping outdoors. What do you think Chip,
should we check them for bugs?!

(Canned laughter)

CHIP: I could send in "The Bug Squad," Bob!

DAN: That isn't funny.

BOB: *(Poking* DAN *in the ribs)* Come on, Dan. We're just
joking around now! Loosen up, buddy! Don't be so
uptight! Try to go with the *flow* a little. Oh! That
reminds me. How about that *room service*, Dan?
That's something, huh? That *room service*? Huh?

DAN: Sure. It's great.

BOB: Call up on the *phone*, ask for something, they bring
it right to you, right up to your room, whatever you
want, as if they worked for *you*, personally.

DAN: Look. I've stayed in good hotels before, if that's
what you're getting at.

(Canned laughter)

BOB: Oh, I'm sure you have Dan. Only the best for the
little *lady*, right?

MAURA: Dan, honey, what are you doing?!

DAN: Well what is *he* doing? He's trying to make fun of
us. I mean we're the guests here!

BOB: *(Whips out a question card)* O K, Dan! What country currently holds the world speed record for the most double cheeseburgers eaten in one hour?

DAN: See? That's not even a real question.

BOB: Of course it's a *real* question, Dan. It's right here on my little card. Who holds the record? Most double cheese-burgers...consumed in an hour.

DAN: We do. O K?

(Canned laughter)

BOB: *(Takes money from DAN)* Maura?

MAURA: Germany?

(Canned laughter)

BOB: *(Takes money from MAURA)* There's no such record.

DAN: I told you.

BOB: Dan! How many days, days on *average*, does it take the Amazonian monitor lizard to complete its annual winter migration across the Serengeti to lay its eggs?

DAN: *(Confused)* Lizards don't migrate.

(Canned applause)

BOB: *(Hands DAN money)* Bingo! Dan, third, and funniest of the ancient Greek tragedians.

DAN: I have no idea.

BOB: *(Takes money from DAN, still facing DAN)* Maura? No? Alright. Maura! Spell entrepreneurial!

MAURA: Uh. O K. O-N-T-R-

(Canned laughter)

BOB: *(Still staring at DAN)* Never mind, Maura. Spell proletariat!

MAURA: Is that an American word, Bob?

DAN: It's Russian.

BOB: Never mind, Maura. Spell "libidinous".

MAURA: Li- what? Li-bid-inous?

(Canned laughter)

BOB: Spell *cat*, Maura.

MAURA: Cat? You mean like a regular cat?

(Canned laughter)

BOB: It's a joke Maura.

MAURA: I don't get it.

(Canned laughter)

BOB: First letter is C.

(Canned laughter)

DAN: Alright, that's it. I don't know what this is supposed to be—

BOB: You don't?

DAN: No. I don't. I've been saying I don't.

BOB: *(Facing out at spectators)* Well, what does it *seem* like it is, Dan?

DAN: What difference does that make?

MAURA: This is how it is, honey. You know that. Remember? We talked about this. This is what he does. He gets you confused. That's the whole first part.

BOB: *(Hands* MAURA *money)* That's right Maura, tell *Dan* how things work here.

MAURA: Like remember the time those people were on, and Bob told that story about a couple of friends of his, and how anal retentive and uptight they were, and they were getting really frustrated and confused and everything and had no idea what was even happening.

And they thought he was talking about *them* the whole time, but then it turned out he wasn't at all, really, and they got all scared and paranoid and everything. That was so funny. Or when those people came on and they didn't tell them anything or what to do at all, and they started to tell all their most intimate *family* things, and they thought they were supposed to, and he was giving them money for it, but then it turned out that they weren't supposed to, and then they just got that year's supply of hair conditioner.

BOB: Well, I'm glad *someone* understands how things work here.

DAN: Look, look, I remember all that. Those people were idiots. This isn't the same thing. We're not even playing! I mean, nothing is even *happening* here, except that he's asking ridiculous questions that don't even *mean* anything, and we're answering them like jerks. And then he makes fun of us for being stupid enough to go along with him and...Jesus, I mean, what kind of a show is that?! I mean, who would want to watch a thing like that?

BOB: Dan, Dan, hello?! Are you with me? What's the problem here exactly, Dan? What's that in your hand there, Dan old buddy? Looks like a big fat wad of *funny money* to me!

DAN: *(Confused, looking at his wad of money)* Yeah, sure, but...O K, right—

MAURA: You're just stopping everything, honey. You're supposed to just let things happen... however they happen. Let's just keep going. It'll be alright in the end, look. *(Waves money at* DAN*)* Come on. Please, Dan?

(Canned applause)

DAN: Oh alright, alright. O K.

BOB: So, do you want to keep *going*?

MAURA: We want to keep going, Bob!

BOB: Dan? It's up to you. Want to keep *going*?

DAN: O K. Alright.

(Canned applause)

BOB: Beautiful! Great! You want to keep going. That's the spirit. See, stick with Maura, Dan. She knows how it works. It's simple. It's like anything. You can't be so thin-skinned and sensitive, Dan...that is, if you want to make it in the *game*. Got to keep your eye on the *prize*, right Maura?

MAURA: *(Waving money)* Right! That's right!

BOB: Yeah, you bet. You just keep playing, playing the *game*, no matter how sick or insane or twisted things seem to get. You just keep fattening that fat wad of *funny money*, and then, in the end, you and Maura can cash in for your *stuff* and live happily ever after.

(Canned applause)

BOB: Stow all those luxury consumer items down there in the hold of that old Greyhound bus, and off you go into the suburban sunset! Roll credits. Now then, where were we? *(Flips through question cards)* Oh, right. O K. Yes or no, Dan, Chinese girls have sideways pussies. Yes or no?

(Pause. BOB and MAURA stare at DAN.)

DAN: Excuse me?

BOB: What, are you deaf, Dan?

DAN: You can't say that. He can't say that, can he?

BOB: I can say anything I want, Dan. It's my show. Haven't I established that?

DAN: But I thought—

BOB: Don't think. Just answer the question.

MAURA: Go ahead, honey. It's probably like some candid camera thing.

DAN: *(To* MAURA*)* You want me to answer that? I can't believe you want me to answer that.

MAURA: Go ahead, honey. It doesn't mean anything.

BOB: That's right, Dan. It's not like it *means* anything.

DAN: I really don't think I want to answer that. I don't. It would be like I was participating—

BOB: Oh grow up, Dan! Be a *man* and answer the question!

MAURA: People say nasty things all the time.

BOB: What are we, little *babies* here, Dan?

DAN: No.

BOB: Good. So answer the question. A. Chinese girls *have* sideways pussies. B. Chinese girls do *not* have sideways pussies.

MAURA: Oh, go ahead, honey. It's just for fun.

DAN: *(Stares at* MAURA *in disbelief for a moment, then answers)* B. O K?

(Canned applause)

BOB: *(Hands* DAN *money)* Yes! B. Of course it's B! What kind of a moron would believe a thing like that? Sideways pussies!

DAN: This is ridiculous.

BOB: O K, true or false, Dan? If you don't vote, you deserve what you get.

MAURA: Just answer. Come on.

DAN: True.

BOB: *(Takes money from* DAN *and* MAURA*)* False! No one deserves what they get, Dan. One more, Dan. What's mayonnaise made out of?

DAN: Uh, eggs, milk, sugar—

(Canned laughter)

BOB: *(Takes money from* DAN*)* Wrong! It's not *made* out of anything, Dan. Mayonnaise is mayonnaise. It just appears in little jars, as if by magic, on the shelves of stores. Just like cars. They just appear there in the showroom in their finished form. That is, unless some nasty little *terrorist*...or some poetic *saboteur*...puts a little *bomb* in there and blows them all up into their component *parts*! Isn't that right, Dan? Unless some slippery little *saboteur* tries to sneak into the *factory* and *deconstruct* everything, tries to turn the *real world* into some kind of *modern art* thing?! Isn't that right?! You have no idea what I'm talking about, do you Dan?

DAN: No.

BOB: No. Of course not. Why would you? Maura! True or false? Yes, or no? Scope kills germs that brushing can't.

MAURA: Yes! Yes, it *does*, Bob!

(Canned applause)

BOB: Absolutely! *(Hands* MAURA *money)* How many *four cylinder* bagels, Dan, in a traditional Bavarian pope-alike festival?!

(Canned laughter)

DAN: In a what? A what?

(Distorted, disturbing variation of theme music plays. Lights flicker, as if an electrical failure were occurring.)

MAURA: *(Cringing, as if to hide from the music)* That's a trick question!

BOB: *(Takes money from* DAN*)* Right or wrong, Dan?! True or false?!

DAN: *(Confused, disoriented by effects)* What? What? What's true or false?

BOB: *(Takes all of* DAN's *money)* Right or wrong, Dan?! Give me an answer!

DAN: It's a trick question, Bob.

BOB: No it's not! Ten seconds!

DAN: Could you repeat the question, Bob?

BOB: No. Five seconds!

DAN: Did you understand the question?

MAURA: Was it something about the Pope?

BOB: Sorry, Dan. Time's all up. And you're out of money. Stand back, Maura.

*(*VERA *enters, holding a truncheon. She rushes at* DAN*.)*

MAURA: Look out Dan!

DAN: What the—

*(*VERA *delivers one savage blow to the back of* DAN's *head with the truncheon.* DAN *collapses onto the floor.* MAURA *screams.* BOB *takes all of* MAURA's *money away and throws it on the floor.* VERA *exits, Music out, lights back to normal. All this happens very fast.)*

DAN: *(Pulling himself up)* Jesus Christ!

BOB: What was that, BLASPHEMER!

MAURA: *(Rushes over to help* DAN *up)* Are you alright, honey?

BOB: *(Grabbing his crotch compulsively)* Right, O K, now we've got a game. Oh, and Maura's got the lead on you, Dan. Time to get serious. Time to get mean. Lots more *funny money* to earn, and plenty of luxurious *consumer items*...to take home with you on the *bus*, Dan!

(Canned laughter)

DAN: What the hell was that all about, Bob?

BOB: *(Reading question card)* O K now, here's a tough one. You're home watching the Carsons. Little Cindy Carson is in the midst of a dilemma. Her little school friends want her to go out after curfew, or smoke a cigarette, or eat pork, or something. Dad's about to give her the big lecture. Suddenly, an ad for a product comes on—

DAN: *(A trickle of blood runs down from his hairline)* Wait! Now, wait, just wait a minute here—

BOB: What's the problem *now*, Dan?

MAURA: Look, you're bleeding!

DAN: The problem? The problem? She... *(Feels his head)* ...uh, that...she just *hit me* with that thing!

BOB: The *thing*? What *thing*?

MAURA: Shhh. Let me see. *(Takes a handkerchief out of DAN's pocket and dabs at wound)*

DAN: The thing, that stick... *(Sees bloody handkerchief, becomes dizzy)* Whoa, now, that's not supposed to happen is it?

BOB: What's the matter? Don't you watch the show at home, Dan?

DAN: Sure I do. But I've never... *(Recoils as MAURA dabs too hard at his head wound)* OWWW! Be careful!

(Canned laughter)

BOB: Dan? Excuse me, Dan. You want to go ahead and make your little point, so we can move on with the show please?

DAN: My little...my little *point*? I'm telling you, that was real. That was a real stick! I don't know what you're trying to do here, Bob. She just wailed on me with a *real* stick!

BOB: Real stick? Nonsense. This is television, Dan.

(Canned laughter)

DAN: I don't care what it is. I'm telling you it was *real*.

MAURA: It *was*, Bob. It was real.

BOB: Look, folks. You know how the show works. That was just Vera, my lovely assistant. Vera's been with the show since the beginning. How many years has it been now, Chip?!

CHIP: Bob, Vera's been with the show *forever*! Vera's been with the show since *day one*, Bob!

BOB: There you go. Vera's been with us forever. Anybody who *watches* the show would know that. It's been me and Vera since way, way back. We work together. We're like a team.

MAURA: *(Dabbing at DAN's head)* It's true, Dan. She's been with the show from the beginning.

DAN: I know that. I know Vera's...that's not what I'm saying. I watch the goddamned show for Christ sakes. Ow! Give me that! *(Takes handkerchief from MAURA, dabs at his head himself)*

(Canned laughter)

MAURA: We watch the show together, Bob.

BOB: Back in Jonestown.

DAN: *Johns*-town. *Johns*-town!

BOB: Uh-huh. So you sit there on your little green couch and eat your little cheeseburgers and watch the show, do you?

MAURA: No, not like that.

BOB: Like what then, Maura? Do you hang suspended from the ceiling and watch?!

MAURA: Well, no, we do sit on the couch but—

BOB: Oh, O K. So you do sit on the couch. And what, you cross the left leg over the right, or is it the right leg over the left? What is it, Maura, are you trying to *bore* us all to death? We're trying to stick to the *point* here, and *get* somewhere, like Dan said he wanted, and *the point*, at the moment, is that you *watch* the *show*. Right?

MAURA: Right.

BOB: Religiously.

MAURA: Well, I don't know—

BOB: It is part of your *routine*! You take it for granted! You depend upon it being there at a certain *time*! It's no longer even a *show*, really, as much as just part of your everyday *reality*. It is something you interact with *unconsciously*, the source of which you have entirely forgotten. It has insinuated itself into the fabric of your life, your everyday life, this subliminal machinery, this show we're talking about, which you claim to watch. *(Continues over* DAN *and* MAURA's *dialog)*

MAURA: This feels wrong.

DAN: I told you. Didn't I?

BOB: You can no longer remember when it first began, nor can you imagine a world without it! *(Continues over* DAN*)*

DAN: *(Holding out bloody handkerchief)* Jesus Christ, look at this, will you!

BOB: Even though you know there was a time...a time when it began, and that it *will* end. Just as it began. Someday it *will* end...as everything that has a beginning ends...even though, *BLASPHEMER*, that whole idea, that whole linear ontological model, becomes impossible at the extremes of either pole, and folds back into itself, collapses into itself, into the little *story* you're telling yourself right now. Which isn't the *point* either. But still, you need it, so you end up measuring backward from *now* to the initial nanosecond which launched the Big Bang, which is so fucking ridiculous it's not even worth commenting on, and is not the *point* either. No, the *point* is, in the *meantime*, while the moments *pass*, you are watching the *show*. You have *always* watched *the show*. Hence, you *know*. You know what happens. You know *exactly* what happens. So what could possibly be the problem?

DAN: The problem? The problem?! You're asking us what's the problem? *(Waving the bloody handkerchief at* BOB*)* Here's the problem right here, Bob!

BOB: What? The hankie? Here, let me see that. *(Shouts out and up as if to the booth)* Uh, excuse me, can we get one of these three-for-a-dollar hankies in here for Dan please!

DAN: No, no. Stop it. You know what I'm saying. Look at this, will you. This is *real blood*, not some fancy talk. And you just tried to change the subject again, but I'm on to you now. Plus, plus, that wasn't even the real *Vera*! What about that?!

MAURA: Right. That's right! It wasn't! He's got you there, Bob.

DAN: The *real* Vera wears a little silver dress, and she's beautiful, and she comes out and shows you things... things you can trade in for. She doesn't come out and beat your head in with a stick, you know? She comes out, the *real* Vera, you know...the lights come up...on a dishwasher or a fridge...or an encyclopedia set or—

(Canned laughter)

BOB: Or a *power* mower?

DAN: Or whatever! Or whatever! Jesus! Forget it!
I don't even know why I'm trying anymore.

BOB: Maybe you folks have been watching the wrong
show.

(Pause)

MAURA: No, no, that's impossible. That's not possible.

BOB: Yeah. You're right. It is impossible. There's only
the *one* show to watch, isn't there? Oh well. I guess we'll
just have to keep at it then, won't we, until whoever is
in charge decides to change it? Oh, and I'd keep at that
head-wound there, Dan. You'll ruin that sporty suit of
yours.

MAURA: But Bob...Dan's right, Bob. That wasn't the real
Vera. That was nothing like her. And the real Vera
doesn't hurt anybody. Dan's right about that. She just
points to the stuff you can win, and...and the real Vera
is pretty, and thin, and that one was, well—

BOB: Maura, Maura, listen to what you're saying, now.
The *real* Vera? The *real* Vera?! Vera is Vera. There is no
real Vera...no *real* Vera and *fake* Vera. Vera is whoever
Vera *is*.

MAURA: Well, Bob, it doesn't look anything like her.

BOB: People look different in real life, Maura.

DAN: Look. Bob. This arguing is stupid. We're big fans
of the show, but, I mean, come on. That...Vera...was a
man...a man in a dress!

MAURA: A man? Are you sure, honey? I don't think it
was a man.

DAN: Yes! Yes, it *was* a man! A big, ugly man in a dress.
(To BOB*)* Look, if you're going to have somebody do
Vera, at least get a woman. I mean, Jesus, Bob, that was

some truck driver in a wig or something. That's not
going to fool anybody. You know that don't you?

BOB: Fool anybody? Why would I want to *fool* anybody,
Dan?

DAN: Would you listen to what I'm saying please?

BOB: I'm trying to Dan, but you're not saying anything
interesting.

MAURA: This is all very, very strange.

DAN: The questions aren't even normal questions.

BOB: Not *normal*?!

DAN: No! I'm sorry, but they're not. And what the hell
is this "*blasphemer*" business? Look, all you're really
doing here is making fun of us, as if we were idiots.
O K, so you're rich and famous and we're not. So we're
just regular people, O K? Average intelligence. So
you're making fun of us. I can understand that, if it's
for entertainment purposes. But this? It's too much.
It's *way* over the top, Bob. I mean, she really hit me.
She really tagged me there. I could've been seriously
hurt, you know. This is the kind of thing some lawyers
I know would just jump all over. You know what I
mean? We could be talking personal injury here.

BOB: *(Pauses)* What are you doing, Dan? Are you
threatening Big Bob?

MAURA: No, Bob, he isn't. Dan, you're not—

BOB: Are you threatening *Big Bob* with litigation?
Is that what you're doing?

DAN: No. O K? I'm sorry. It's just that you're standing
there like normal trying to tell us that everything is O K.

BOB: When did I ever say everything was O K? When
did I ever say that, Dan?

DAN: Just now! Just now! You said that was Vera.

BOB: It is.

DAN: Like hell!

MAURA: Dan! Don't.

BOB: Are you calling Big Bob a liar, Dan?

DAN: No. All I'm saying...I'm just saying that that *guy*...wasn't the real Vera. That's all I'm saying. You can say whatever you want, Bob, and you can say it over and over and over, but I know what I saw. I saw what I saw.

BOB: Listen, Dan. I'm going to explain this again. I know this is hard for you, but try to stay with me. See, this is *California*. Things are just a bit more *sophisticated* than the gasket business. O K? There is no *real* Vera. Vera is just a name...for the girl on the show. She's a character we made up. Vera could be whoever, understand? There is no *real* Vera. There is no *fake* Vera. So, if I say that was Vera, then that was Vera. On account of I'm the one running things here. Is that clear enough? I think it is. When you go and get your *own* show, Dan, then you can say who's Vera, and who is not Vera. Until then, Dan, while you're here in *my* show, Vera is whoever the fuck I say she is.

(Canned laughter)

DAN: No, no, no, no...you can't just say that. That's not what I meant—

MAURA: Well, Vera or no Vera, no one said anything about any hitting, Bob! Dan's got a point there.

DAN: Hold on a second, honey.

BOB: No, let her talk Dan. She has a right to talk. She may have—

DAN: No Bob, she interrupted *me*! Don't tell me what to let my wife do or not do!

BOB: Dan. Dan! What did we just say about talking when I'm talking? You just cut me off in the middle of a sentence.

MAURA: And I was going to say, there isn't even any stuff. There's real hitting and no prizes!

DAN: That's what I was saying before you piped in.

MAURA: Well, I didn't know. Am I supposed to read your mind?!

DAN: Could I *finish*, please? Do you think I could *finish*?! Thank you very much. *(To* BOB*)* O K, Bob, shouldn't there be like a display case back there with all the stuff in it...and Vera comes out and lights up the little boxes one by one?! I mean, if this is the *real* Big Bob show, then where's all the stuff? We're the *guests*! Here we are! We're playing the *game*! We're trying to anyway. And we've been standing here trying to keep up and follow you, and give the right answers. And we've been good sports. So where are the prizes?! Is this what we get...our heads bashed in? How does that make sense?!

BOB: You know, you're really very rude to your mother, uh, wife, Dan. Really very rude. You know you don't have to take that from him.

MAURA: He doesn't mean anything by it, Bob. He just gets—

DAN: Stop it. Don't change the subject! Stop changing the subject!

BOB: O K. I'm sorry. What was it you wanted, Dan? Some kind of display case...full of products somewhere...a display case full of luxury consumer items?

DAN: No, no—

MAURA: Can I say something please?

DAN: What?! What?!

MAURA: I just realized something. This is not even the normal place where the show is. I just realized that now. I know the set changes, but it's more than that. I don't even think it's the right building. Now, maybe you changed the whole show or something, which is your right to do, and we certainly understand how competitive everything is these days, and maybe some people wouldn't mind getting hit...if it's part of the game. But, you see, Bob, we don't go in for hitting, or anything like that. Not even when it's watching other people get hit...people we don't know, because they're dumb or whatever...and they deserve to get hit. I mean, some people do. But we don't even like to watch the police shows or anything, or the violent movies, or the wars, or anything. I know it's good for ratings, and it's not like we're Quakers, but we just don't enjoy it. We don't find it entertaining. We're against it, basically, violence and cruelty, and we think there's way too much of it, Bob. There is, you know, all the hitting and shooting and everybody raping and beating each other up. It's awful, Bob. And the kids see it all. It can't be good for them, can it, to see that?

BOB: (Sighs wearily) No, of course it can't be good for them, Maura. Gosh, after a while they might begin to think that the world consists of nothing but these brutal, selfish people who'd do anything for a buck.

MAURA: Right. Right! That's what I'm saying!

BOB: U-huh. O K. So, let me ask you then, what *do* you want to do *here*? Tonight, I mean. Not this, obviously. What, then? Hmm? Just sit around and talk? Talk to each other? Is that what you had in mind, folks? Sit around and whine like a bunch of aristocrats? A bunch of *Russian* aristocrats maybe? No? Oh, I know. Was there some kind of *story* you wanted to tell, some *story* we haven't already heard... already heard a thousand

times? Could it be the *story* of your troubled childhood,
or of someone *else's* troubled childhood? Some tragic
story about somebody's *son*? O K. We could try that,
I guess. I'm sure the folks at home would love to see
that. I'm sure they're just dying to hear every last detail
of your *personal problems* in dramatic form!

(Canned laughter. MAURA *bursts into tears, rushes to* DAN.
DAN *comforts her.)*

BOB: No? Alright. What then? Hmm. Shall we air out
some sort of grievance you might have? How about it?
Dan? Maura? No? Some type of *social grievance* you'd
like to share? Consider yourselves representatives
of some *oppressed minority*, poor *white trash*, perhaps?
Like to blow off some steam?

(Canned laughter, faint, shrill feedback over P A)

BOB: Wait, did I just say white trash? I'm sorry, actually,
I meant the *middle class*, whose views I represent, of
course. Oh, wait, better yet, I tell you what we'll do.
We'll just forget all that *heavy* stuff, and just watch
ourselves a *ball game*. How about it, Dad, uh, Dan,
I mean? No? Shit. O K, well, how about a nice, peaceful
game of checkers then? The folks at home will just *love*
watching that! That'll just entertain the shit out of folks.
We'll just move the little pieces around... around and
around in the lights all night... and see what pretty
patterns they happen to make. It'll be, uh, *abstract*,
or *conceptual*, or whatever. Or wait, hold on now,
I just remembered. I think we've got a tape of the meek
inheriting the earth we could run. How about it, Chip?
Do we have that tape?!

CHIP: We've got that tape cued up and ready to roll,
Bob!

BOB: We've got a "meek inheriting the earth" tape,
Chip?!

CHIP: Oh, I'm sorry. I thought you said the "rags to riches" tape, Bob.

BOB: What about that "pulling yourself up by your own bootstraps" tape, Chip?

CHIP: Oh, that's a good one, Bob! I think we've got *that* one.

BOB: How about that "King Dan gets it up the ass with a Russian saber" tape, Chip?!

CHIP: What ever you say, Bob!

(Feedback rises. MAURA, becomes disoriented, wanders around, staring blankly.)

DAN: Now, Bob. Bob. Look, let's stop this. Seriously. Maura is upset. She's...look...now, it was our understanding that—

(Feedback drops out.)

BOB: *Your* understanding. *(Laughing)* Listen to yourself. *Your* understanding. Your understanding of what, Dan?

DAN: Bob, Bob...now, here's the thing—

BOB: You don't even know what you're trying to say, do you? You just open your mouth and the words come out and as long as you can hear the sound of your own voice then you think you're saying something. But in fact, Dan, you don't really *have* anything to say, do you? Nothing to say at all. Do you? But you're not going to let *that* stop you, are you, Dan? You're going to keep talking regardless, aren't you? Yes. You are. Why? I'll tell you. Because you're fucking incapable of keeping your fucking mouth shut and letting somebody else who may, in fact, *have* something to say, say something. Isn't that how it is, Dan?

DAN: No!

BOB: Yes! That *is* how it is. That is *exactly* how it is.
Isn't that how it is, Chip?

CHIP: Right *again*, Bob! That's *exactly* how it is, and how
it's *always* been, from time immemorial!

BOB: I'm sorry, when was that exactly, Chip?

CHIP: From the dawn of time, Bob, when the first
proto-humans crawled out of the filthy stinking slime
and started scratching squiggly symbols into those cave
walls in France!

BOB: France?!

CHIP: That's right, Bob, PARIS, FRANCE!

MAURA: Is this going out? Are people even seeing this?

DAN: Shut up Maura.

BOB: Yeah. You tell her, Dan.

DAN: No. Hold on a minute—

BOB: *(Explodes)* No, you hold on, Dan! *(Quickly regains
composure, clears throat)* Alright, now, I'm getting the
feeling that you folks are not entirely satisfied with
how the show is going at the moment. I'm getting that
feeling rather distinctly, what with all these complaints,
and how neither of you, *neither* of you, has even so
much as bothered to ring your little buzzers when you
answer questions, which will cost you, believe me.

DAN: Buzzers? What buzzers?

BOB: What buzzers?! *(Presses buttons on contestant
podiums, causing shrill buzzer sounds)* These buzzers!
They're right here in fucking front of you, folks!
We must be an hour into the goddamn show, and no
goddamn buzzers! Do we have a count on that, Chip?

CHIP: We're at forty eight minutes and twenty seven
seconds, Bob!

BOB: Forty eight minutes and twenty seven seconds... and no fucking buzzers! *(Drops rage flat)* And you know, I'm hurt. Can I tell you that? I mean, we invite you folks out here, set you up in a nice hotel, meals, room service, and then you come on the show and act like a couple of... Now, I'm getting the sense that you don't approve of the way I'm doing things here. In fact, my sense is that you've been sitting there thinking how easy it would be to *replace* me entirely...as if I didn't exist at all, and had never existed, and forget all about me. You denied it before, but it is what you're thinking. Isn't that what you've been thinking, Dan? Isn't that exactly what you'd like to do? Big Dan the Gasket Man?! The Big Fat Dan Show...with Vera his lovely fucking assistant?

DAN: No.

BOB: Come on! It's what you want!

MAURA: Honey—

DAN: I said no.

BOB: What is *wrong* with you? You've obviously come to the startling conclusion that I'm not running things the way they're *supposed* to be run. Isn't that right, Dan? I'm not playing the *game*, or *whatever*, the way the it was *meant* to be played? Well, in order to come to such a conclusion, one must, *necessarily*, have *some* idea as to how the game is *supposed* to be played. Which means that you have some *model* in your head that you're comparing this to, and it's not matching up. You came in here with some unconscious preconception of what *is* and what *is not* acceptable. So fine. Here's your chance. Why don't you come on up here, Dan, and show us how things are *supposed* to go...how it's supposed to be done...what's supposed to happen? Why don't you do that, since you're so fucking *knowledgeable*, and you know exactly what is *wrong* with everything, and everyone, everywhere, and precisely how to *fix* it all. Which is understandable, that you would think this way, Dan, when one considers what a fucking swell job you have done so far, with the world, I mean. Isn't that right, Dad, uh, Dan, I mean?

MAURA: *(Disoriented, off in another world)* Don't fight boys, please. Not now.

BOB: This is between me and Dan, Maura.

MAURA: We came to play, not to fight

BOB: Made quite a *name* for yourself, have you, Dan? Big Dan, the *sales* man? Emperor Dan?! Mister fucking Science with all your fancy little *machines*?! Oh, whoops! I forgot, you don't have any little *machines*! There's no *machinery*...no *process* here at all...nothing to question or wonder about at all!

MAURA: *(Disoriented, staring out at imaginary camera)* Why aren't there any commercials, Bob?

BOB: Reality just grows on trees, right Dan? And you're just in there from the beginning, aren't you. It's not manufactured. It's real. Right, Dan?

DAN: I don't know what you're talking about.

BOB: You are goddamn right you don't.

MAURA: Bob?

BOB: What?!

MAURA: *(Still staring out)* Aren't we going to break for a commercial?

BOB: *(Staring at DAN)* No, Maura, actually, we're *not*. We're actually not going to break for a commercial. And don't you want to know why, Maura?

MAURA: I guess I do...want to know why, Bob.

BOB: Tell her why, Chip.

CHIP: Well, Maura, there's really no *need* to break for a commercial, because from this moment on the show itself is just one *big* commercial that never ends! One big commercial from now to eternity!

BOB: There you go, Maura. One big commercial, from now to eternity, forever and ever. And why is it one big commercial, Dan? By *accident*? No. Because we designed it that way.

MAURA: I wonder what it is we're selling.

BOB: Unless I'm *lying*, which I could be, right, Chip?

CHIP: No, Bob, I'm sorry, but no. You could *not* be lying!

BOB: *(Still staring at* DAN*)* And why is that, Chip?

CHIP: Well Bob, because I'm afraid that would imply an a priori concept of *Truth*, from which one could deviate, rather than the *word* "Truth" being merely a machinic element within technologies of *power*, which have been set into motion by certain *(Clears throat)* unnamed and unnameable parties, which just coincidentally happens to be the case here, Bob.

BOB: Yes. Precisely. Thank you, Chip. But, hey, you know, if I *am* in charge, I could break my own rules, theoretically, couldn't I? I mean, I could be *lying* in relation to the truth which I made up previously, which would also be a lie, so that by deviating from it I would make it true, so that I'd be telling the truth by lying. Couldn't I be telling the *truth* by *lying*? What do you think, Dan, right or wrong?

(Brief pause)

DAN: You know, Bob, I have no idea what the hell you're talking about. And now that I think about it, I really couldn't tell you what the hell is even going on here. And you know what else? I don't care. See, whatever it is you're trying to do, it doesn't have anything to do with me, or with Maura either, or with people like us. Look, obviously, you've got some kind of problem, some deep-seated psychological problem, that you need to work out, that doesn't have anything to do us. We came here to have *fun*, and *play*, and *enjoy* ourselves, and, I mean, what *is* this?! O K, fine, so you're all worked up over...whatever the hell it is you're worked up over. But we're not. We're *fine*. We don't *need* this. Right now we could be out, uh—

MAURA: *(Still staring out, disoriented)* Shopping.

DAN: What?

BOB: Shopping, Dan. Right or wrong?

DAN: Maura! Get over here!

(Distorted theme music up and lights flicker as before. MAURA is shocked out of her stupor by the effects, and tries to rush to DAN. BOB blocks her path.)

BOB: *(Spins around towards DAN)* I said, Right or Wrong, Dan?!

(VERA enters, rushes at DAN with the truncheon. DAN retreats to his podium. VERA hesitates, hovers over him with the truncheon.)

BOB: Right or wrong! Agree Disagree! Right Left! Yes No! Good Bad! With us or against us!

MAURA: Oh God! What's happening? Dan! Dan!

DAN: *(Cowering at his podium, as VERA hovers over him)* I don't know! Right! Good! Whatever!

BOB: Use your fucking buzzer!

DAN: *(Presses buzzer repeatedly)* Yes! No! Get her away from me! Jesus Christ!

(VERA exits. BOB releases MAURA. She rushes to DAN's side. Music out and lights back to normal. DAN is still pounding his buzzer. Canned applause)

BOB: *(Throwing money on the floor at Dan's feet)* Now then, that wasn't so hard, was it? See how simple everything can get? You can stop ringing your buzzer now, Dan. Right, uh, where were we, Chip?

CHIP: Maybe we ought to tell the Browns what they're playing for, Bob!

BOB: Yeah, yeah, sure. Tell them what they're playing for.

CHIP: It's a *NEW CAR!!!*

(Canned applause)

BOB: Oh, Christ. Still the new car?

CHIP: Yes, I'm afraid so, Bob. It's that *new car* again.

BOB: Jesus Christ. Hasn't anybody *won* that damn thing yet?

CHIP: I'm afraid not, Bob. It's still here in the *show*room, gathering dust, zero on the odometer.

BOB: Really.

CHIP: That's right, Bob. Brand new car. All fueled up. Fully loaded. Here for the taking. Ready to go.

(DAN and MAURA stare at BOB, in shock.)

BOB: *(Sadly)* Alright. How about it then? Dan? Maura? Anybody? Brand new car? No? No car? Oh, come on folks, we've got a *show* to do. Dan? Maura? Hello? Hello?! Whoops, I think we're losing them, Chip. Hello? Maura? Bob to Maura! Come in Maura!

MAURA: What, Bob?

DAN: *(Hugging MAURA, turning her away from BOB)* Get away from us.

BOB: I was just saying, uh, asking rather, you give good head then, do you Maura?

MAURA: Give what?

BOB: Head? Go down, you know, like... *(Pantomimes fellatio, hand to mouth, tongue in cheek)* Hey, where's my laugh track?

MAURA: *(Nearly faints)* Oh dear lord—

DAN: *(Sits MAURA down, comes around the podium at BOB)* Alright. That's enough. I've had it with you. I don't have to take this! We don't have to take this.

BOB: Go back to your place, Dan.

DAN: No. I won't. I don't care who you are. That's my goddamn *wife* you're talking to asshole.

(Canned laughter)

MAURA: Dan, don't.

DAN: *(Lunges for BOB)* You can't talk to her like that!

BOB: *(Evades DAN)* Oh. O K.

(Distorted music up. Lights flicker. VERA enters, rushes at DAN with truncheon.)

DAN: *(Spins around to defend himself)* Come on, you son of a—

MAURA: Don't, honey!

(VERA beats DAN savagely.)

BOB: Yeah, you get her, Dan.

MAURA: Stop! Stop!

BOB: Yeah, you give her what for, Dan old buddy. Show her who's who. Teach her a lesson. No justice, no peace...ah yes. Great. Brilliant. I can't wait for the reviews.

(Music out, lights normal as VERA exits. DAN on the floor, moaning in agony.)

BOB: Oh well, so much for the old fighting spirit. Where were we? Oh right. What about you, Dan? Head south a bit, do you?

MAURA: *(Drags* DAN *back to his chair)* This is not right.

BOB: I said, what about you, Dan?

MAURA: He's not playing anymore.

BOB: Sure he is. Come on.

MAURA: This is not right.

BOB: Oh bullshit, Maura. You're loving this.

MAURA: No! I'm not. I am *not* loving this!

BOB: Oh, I see, can't abandon Dan yet. Sacred vows. Uh-huh. Right. So, what is it, Dan's not *playing* anymore? Dan Dan not play anymore? Dan Dan hurt his noggy woggin?

MAURA: Honey...I think maybe we should *leave*, honey.

DAN: *(Badly disoriented)* Give me a minute. My ears... I can't—

BOB: Excuse me, but we're still *playing*, Dan. We're still playing the *game*, on account of how Maura insists on pretending this isn't what she wants...that this isn't what she's been wanting forever. So we'll have to keep *playing*. Now then, where were we? Oh yes. Which is it, Dan? Do you go *down*, or what, you think it smells funny? Let's go, Dan. Respond to the stimulus. What, am I going to have to get Vera back out here?

MAURA: Wait, he's going to answer! Please—

BOB: *(Turning away, checking his watch)* Just answer the fucking question already.

MAURA: You better answer him, honey. Come on.

DAN: *(Mutters)* No. Fuck him.

BOB: *(Staring out at spectators)* I'm sorry, Dan, I don't believe I heard your answer.

DAN: *(To BOB)* I said, fuck you!

BOB: Fuck me? *(Laughs briefly, sadly)* Fuck me? That's good. Yeah, that's the old Dan I used to know and love. Your making me nostalgic for the old days now.

(Distorted music up. Lights flicker. VERA re-enters, beats DAN mercilessly. MAURA screams, flails at VERA. DAN curls up into a ball on the floor. Finally, VERA backs off, and exits. Music out, lights normal)

MAURA: *(Trying to pull DAN up)* Let's go Dan. Let's go now! Before he starts again.

DAN: I can't move right now.

BOB: Oh, you're quitting on me too now, Maura? I don't think so.

MAURA: C'mon honey, let's go back home.

BOB: You mean to the *hotel.*

MAURA: To the hotel. Right.

DAN: *(Delirious)* Can we order Wendy's? I'm dying for a Wendy's.

MAURA: Whatever you want, honey. Just get up now.

DAN: *(Ordering from the drive-through)* I'll take a double...a double with extra pickles please.

BOB: Tough guy, huh? Going to teach us a lesson... teach us all a lesson about right and wrong.

MAURA: I think we should leave right *now*, Dan. I don't think it's ever going to stop.

DAN: I can't walk right now. Give me a minute.

BOB: Big shot gasket salesman. Come in here...going to show old Bob and Vera how to run things. Doesn't want to answer my questions anymore.

MAURA: *(Exploding at* BOB*)* Oh, you're in trouble! You're in big, big trouble. This is so wrong I can't even believe how wrong it is!

BOB: Wrong? What's wrong about it? I thought you wanted to *win* things?

MAURA: We did! We did! We *did* want to win things!

BOB: Well, you can't win if you don't *play*! What, you think we're going to just *give* the stuff away?!

MAURA: There's nothing to win. There's nothing to win!

BOB: What are you talking about? There's plenty of stuff to win. What about that new car?

MAURA: Well, where is it then? Where is it?! I don't see it!

BOB: We'll give it to you later.

MAURA: Give to us *now*! Give it to us *now*!

BOB: Maura, you're hysterical.

MAURA: Give it to us *now*!

BOB: I can't. In your state, you're liable to wreck it. Plus, you haven't earned it yet.

MAURA: What about Dan?! Look at him! Look! Don't we deserve something for that?

BOB: For what, getting the snot beat out of him? Dan broke the rules. He has to learn the hard way.

MAURA: But there are no rules! You said no rules!

BOB: So I lied. I can lie. It's my show, right? Come on now, Maura, what are you going to do, go around for the rest of your life resenting me because I lied a little.

Fine. O K. I know a couple shrinks you'll probably want to talk to. *(Reaching inside coat)* I've got their cards here somewhere, I think.

(Canned laughter)

BOB: But seriously, Maura, can we be adults here? Do you want to keep playing...playing the *game*? It's up to you. It's all up to you.

DAN: *(Rising, pulling himself up on* MAURA*)* Maura, don't talk to him. That's how he gets you. Don't even listen to him.

BOB: Dan's right, Maura, don't even listen to me. Stare at the ceiling. Pretend it isn't happening.

DAN: *(On his feet, leaning on* MAURA*)* O K, let's go.

BOB: Uh, I'd stay down if I were you, Dan.

MAURA: *(Trying to support* DAN's *weight)* We're leaving. We're going. We don't want your *cars* and your *money* and *things*. We don't need them!

BOB: Oh, I'm afraid you do.

DAN: *(Slipping down)* Honey, wait—

(Canned laughter)

BOB: *(Laughs)* Where exactly do you think you're going?

DAN: *(Slipping, clutching* MAURA*)* Don't answer him... Maura, I'm slipping here.

*(*MAURA *circles, looking for a way out, trying to hold* DAN *up.* DAN *slips further and further down.)*

MAURA: I'm sorry, Bob, but you'll have to find someone else.

BOB: There isn't anyone else, Maura.

DAN: I'm slipping...Maura!

MAURA: *(Losing him)* I've got you, Dan.

BOB: This is just pathetic. Will both of you please go back to your little podiums before I lose my patience entirely?

(DAN *slips to the floor.*)

MAURA: *(Trying to pull DAN up)* Dan! Dan!

BOB: *(Mutters under his breath)* This is never going to work.

(BOB *signals up toward the control booth. Distorted music. Lights flicker.* VERA *re-enters, beats DAN brutally.*)

MAURA: *(Fighting VERA off)* No! No! Get back! Bad!

BOB: *(Checking his watch)* You see what happens.

MAURA: Stop her! God!

BOB: *(Flat, monotone)* Stop. Stop.

MAURA: *(Pushing VERA away)* Get off! God help us! Get off! Bad!

BOB: *(Flat, monotone)* Oh God please help them.

MAURA: Please! Please! Dan! Get up!

BOB: *(Yawning)* Ten points, Dan.

(Canned applause)

MAURA: You have to get it up, Dan! Dan! Oh God! Stop it! Bad Vera! Jesus! You're killing him! You're going to kill him!

BOB: Fifty points, Dan.

(MAURA *abandons* DAN, *runs down and, facing spectators, shouts out at imaginary camera.*)

MAURA: Help us! Please! Won't somebody help us! Big Bob is killing Dan!

(Canned laughter)

MAURA: Are these cameras on? Hello! Hello! This is
Maura Brown from Johnstown, Pennsylvania! We're
here on the Big Bob show and something has gone
wrong.

(Canned laughter)

MAURA: We got off track somehow, in the beginning,
I think, and we've been trying to fix it but it just hasn't
worked! They won't let us win and they won't let us
leave and now we're stuck in here with Bob and Vera
and it's all one big commercial and the cars...help! For
God's sake, please...this is not part of the show! This is
really happening! Listen to me! Listen...

*(Music out. BOB applauds MAURA's speech. Lights normal.
VERA exits. MAURA on her knees, weeps silently. DAN
crawls around in circles in a stupor, reaching up into the
air blindly. MAURA crawls toward DAN.)*

BOB: All done talking to yourself, Maura? What did you
think, I was just going to let you run out on me? I've got
a *show* to do. I've got *responsibilities*. Do you have any
idea how much *money* is tied up in this thing, *invested*
in this whole setup?! Do you have any idea?!

MAURA: *(Crawling to DAN)* No! No!

BOB: No, of course you don't. No. How could you?

MAURA: *(Trying to restrain DAN)* Be still, honey.

BOB: Nice little couple from Hicksville, Pennsylvania.
Or was that Hicksville, New York?

DAN: Get the dog!

BOB: Nice little couple, that never hurt nobody.

MAURA: Shh, honey...don't try to talk.

BOB: Do you know what a *sponsor* is? Do you, Maura?
Well, a sponsor is somebody who *invests*...in an

enterprise. And a sponsor can be an *individual,* or a group of individuals.

MAURA: *(Focusing on* DAN*)* O K, whatever. Whatever. Whatever.

BOB: Ever heard of the L P T Group of Companies, Maura?

DAN: Maura?

MAURA: Yes, it's *me,* Dan.

BOB: It's a rather large concern...millions of shareholders...regular folks, just like yourselves.

MAURA: Do you know where you are, honey?

BOB: Maura?

MAURA: What?!

BOB: Have you ever heard of The L P T Group of *Companies,* Maura?!

MAURA: No! Damn you! Can't you *stop* for one minute?!

BOB: No. I can't. Pay attention when I'm talking to you.

MAURA: Listen. Bob. I think Dan's really hurt. I think there's something wrong with his head.

BOB: We're talking about a really huge *investment* here. Millions. Billions. Trillions of dollars. Invested in this *undertaking,* Maura.

MAURA: I've got to get him to a doctor, Bob.

BOB: Ever seen a million dollars? A billion dollars? Stacked up in little rows, neat little rows, in a shiny leather briefcase? Like your *Dad* used to carry? How much do you figure your life is worth, compared to a billion American dollars?

MAURA: Please, please listen to me.

BOB: I'm talking a trillion...a gazillion dollars...a billion gazillion...moving at lightning speed, through little fiber optic telephone lines. I'm talking a lot of fucking money. I'm talking life-styles of the rich and famous... exotic ports of call...immunity from prosecution!

CHIP: A brand new *car*!

BOB: Atlantic fucking City, Maura! Hong Kong prostitutes! Rivers of oil! The south of France! The whole transnational magilla! I'm talking about what makes the world go 'round! I'm talking ratings! Advertising dollars!

MAURA: Bob?

BOB: Are you *listening* to me? I'm trying to help you.

MAURA: Bob. I think we ought to stop the show. I think Dan needs a doctor, now.

BOB: Stop the *show*?!

MAURA: He's hurt real bad, Bob.

BOB: Well of course he's hurt, Maura. Look at his head. Vera just beat the shit out of him with a bat. He's probably got brain damage at the very least. What, so you think we ought to just stop the whole *show* so we can take poor Dan to see a brain doctor? What do you say, Dan? How's the *brain*?!

DAN: Are we rained out, Pop?

BOB: Nope, afraid not, boy. Game's still on! It's the *train*, son. You missed the goddamn *train*! They left without you. Now you're fucked.

MAURA: Stop it.

BOB: But hey, tell you what. Why don't you just hang around *here* for a while, Dan. Sell some gaskets to the locals and all. You can get the *next* train, if there ever is one.

DAN: I'll get the seven 'o two, Pop.

MAURA: Shhh, honey. It's alright. Don't talk.

BOB: Yeah, you do that, Dan. Get that seven 'o two.
Now what the hell were we talking about anyway?
Oh right, investment in the superstructure. And all
the nice people who are making that investment,
or have made that investment, or are—

(MAURA, *snaps, rushes at* BOB *and tries, feebly, to assault*
him, slapping at him, beating his chest. He gets hold of her
and restrains her quickly, embracing her, smiling, laughing.
Once restrained, her rage dissolves into tears.)

BOB: *(Laughing)* Now, you really shouldn't have done
that, Maura.

MAURA: *(Weeping, broken)* I want you to stop this and let
us out of here. I want you to let us out of here right now.

BOB: *(Turns and walks away)* Sure, sure.

MAURA: This has gone far enough.

BOB: You really shouldn't have done that, Maura...
Maura Brown, from, where was it, *Kent, Ohio?*

MAURA: You're in big trouble, Bob. Big, big trouble.
Everything you did...is on T V, and everyone saw
it...saw everything...what you did to Dan...and
everything...and the world...the whole world is
watching...the whole world is watching...watching
what you do...they're watching it all...and people
won't stand for it.

BOB: No, Maura, I suppose you're right. People won't
stand by and just let it happen. I see that now. No, of
course not. They'll see what's going on, and they'll
make the connections...about how this relates...to things
that are happening...in the *real* world, that is, and they'll
feel that they have to, I don't know, change their whole
value systems...their entire lives...just change everything,

radically. Sure. Right. Of course they will. They'll have this mind-blowing moment of clarity and march right out of this building tonight and start changing the world. They'll cash out of the market, quit their jobs, and take to the streets, give everything they have to the poor and the hungry, change the whole world. Is that the general idea?

MAURA: Right. Yes. No. I don't know. I don't know... I don't know what we're supposed to do.

BOB: *(Blatantly ironic)* Yeah. Me neither. I'm totally in the dark. Oh, well. I guess we'll just have to continue then. *(Calls offstage)* Oh Vera darling! You want to get in here please and continue beating the shit out of Dan?! It seems that Maura doesn't know what to do.

*(*VERA *re-enters, beats* DAN *savagely, but without enthusiasm, looking exasperated.)*

BOB: In fact, it seems that *no-one* knows. It seems we're all completely in the dark here. It seems we're all trapped here in a world we didn't *make*, and have no *control* over whatsoever. Yes, it's a big fucking existential mystery...a big fucking mystery that we can never solve.

*(*DAN *moans briefly, then loses consciousness.* MAURA *throws herself down at* BOB's *feet.* VERA *beats* DAN's *unconscious body.)*

MAURA: O K, no, I'm sorry. Please, God, I'll do anything...make her stop please...Bob...please... I'll do anything you want.

BOB: Why don't you try threatening me some more, Maura? Maybe that'll help. Threatening to punish me...to hold me to account. Or what about insults? Harsh language. That could work. You could sit around with your friends and call me *names*. Or maybe you could get together and, you know, occupy the *studio*, or wherever we are. Oh, I know what, why don't you call what's his name, Abbie Hoffman, and get him to come down here and call Big Bob a pig? Whoops, but he's *dead*! Isn't he?! Funny. Or maybe you could just scream into the cameras some more about how Big Bob is killing everyone and ruining everything. You could spend a serious amount of time on that, getting the "anti-Bob" *message* out there...out to the people! We could arrange for a *babysitter* to free you up for that, so you could go down and march, or...oh Jesus! What am I thinking?! You don't *need* a babysitter, do you, Maura? And plus, I've got my decades all screwed up again! Damn! I do that, get things all mixed up. Decades. Generations. Space. Time. Freedom. Love. Hate. History. It's all so relative. Things. Aren't they? They're like a big beet salad inside my brain.

MAURA: I'm sorry. I'm sorry. Just tell me what you want. I'll do whatever...anything you want.

BOB: Yes. I think we've established that, Maura.

(VERA *stops beating* DAN *and stands there.* BOB *crosses downstage.* MAURA *crawls to* DAN. VERA *exits during* BOB's *speech.*)

BOB: The problem is...what the hell do I want? I can't, for the life of me...I can't seem to remember. I mean, there should be something that I want, shouldn't there, that would explain all this. But what could Bob want that he doesn't already have? Let's see, he's got a house and servants and cars and T Vs and planes and boats and artwork and money and women and clothes and beliefs and stock and dishwashers and facts and, well, we could just go on forever. What is it that Bob does *not* have? Jesus, I just can't think of it. Seems like everything. Got my own *T V show*. People come on... do pretty much whatever I tell them. I tell them to show up at a specific time, they show up at that time, just like magic. I tell them what to wear. That's what they wear.

I give them money, cars, things. They thank me. They don't ask a lot of questions. I tell them to be for, or against, something. They are. It's as simple as that, normally. They don't really care if it makes any sense. They're just grateful to be here, and not get hit. Most people, anyway.

MAURA: *(Muttering, in tears)* They're going to get you.

BOB: Who is, Maura? Who is going to get me? Hey, Chip?

CHIP: Yes, Bob?

BOB: You didn't see the *Pope* out there in the parking lot on your way in, did you?

CHIP: No, Bob. I didn't. As a matter of fact.

BOB: Didn't see *Genghis Khan* out there...lining up his Mongol hordes?

CHIP: I looked around pretty well, Bob, but no.

BOB: Trotsky? You didn't happen to see Trotsky out there?

CHIP: No, Bob. Sorry, but the only folks I saw out there were a lot of *contestant types* trying to get *into* the show so they could play the *game* and win some *stuff.*

BOB: And you showed them the pictures of how they're supposed to look and talk?

CHIP: That's right, Bob, showed them the pictures, gave out the little handbooks, the whole nine yards.

DAN: *(Comes to suddenly, sits bolt upright)* Starsky!

MAURA: *(Rushes to DAN)* Dan!

BOB: Uh, that was *Trotsky*, Dan, but hey...whatever.

MAURA: *(Holding DAN)* Don't move honey. The police are coming.

BOB: Trotsky, Starsky. Who gives a fuck? Drink fucking Coke! Obey your fucking thirst! Life's a *sport*, right?! Sure it is. At least for *most* people, right, Chip?

CHIP: Right again, Bob! I don't know how you do it! It's nothing short of preternatural!

BOB: Of course there are always going to be a few *losers* around, a few *sissies* around, who want to ruin everything, on account of they're not tough enough to handle the *competition*. But they're a tiny, insignificant minority. So fuck them, right Dan?

DAN: *(Delirious)* Right, Pop...fuck 'em.

(DAN collapses. MAURA runs to him, lifts him, cradles him in her lap.)

BOB: Right. I mean, the vast *majority* of people are good, decent, hard working Americans...with *investments*, and loans, who are in there every day...competing, fighting, clawing their way up the ladder...playing hard...playing to *win*. Am I right, or am I right? I'm talking about people who would be *grateful* just to be here, to have the chance to be here where you are. Don't you realize where we are, Maura? I mean, look around. Jesus. Fuck. We're *here*. This is *it*. We made it. We're *home*. This is where it's been heading all along, all these thousands of years of evolution, wars, philosophies, religions, cultures, civilizations, scientific inquiry, all struggling toward *this* one great goal. All recorded human history, all leading *here*, to this...to us. Look at it! Isn't it fucking beautiful, folks?! Look around! Blue fucking skies! Top of the World, Ma! What do you want? Money? *(Throws handfuls of funny money around)* Here. We got *money* coming out our asses here. We got it all. We got everything here. What do you want, *consumer* items?! Fine. Whatever. Why didn't you say so? Shit, I mean, if there's anything we've got, it's an inexhaustible supply of *consumer* items...of every conceivable shape, size and

color. Oh fuck yes we've got everything here. We got it
all. Shit, whoa, my mind is staggered by the magnitude
of it. I can't even think. Help me out here. What else
have we got, Chip?

CHIP: You mean, besides the consumer items, Bob?

BOB: Yeah. Besides the consumer items.

CHIP: Well, there's the *money*.

BOB: O K. Great. So we've got the consumer items and
we've got the money. What else have we got back there
in the back, Chip?

CHIP: Uh, that's pretty much *it*, Bob.

BOB: That's *it*? The consumer items and the money and
that's it? Are you sure, Chip?

CHIP: Uh, yeah, Bob. That's it.

BOB: Hey, well...that's enough, isn't it? I mean, what
else could a person possibly *want*? You got your *money*
and you got your *consumer* items. What else is there?
Speak of the devil...

(VERA *re-enters, arms full of commodities—toasters,
ashtrays, lamps, anything—and drops them in front of*
DAN *and* MAURA. MAURA, *in shock, stares at them as
if they were human heads.*)

BOB: Look, here they are. Here, we got some *products*
for you. All kinds of products. Nice shiny products
They're all yours, folks. Here, what's this? Who cares?
Whatever. Take it. Here you go. Take them home.
Eat them. Sell them. Shove them up your ass. Who
gives a fuck?

(BOB *sifts through the pile of commodities and money,
stuffing things into* MAURA'*s hands.* VERA *exits and
returns with more products.* MAURA *tries to cradle* DAN
in her lap, but BOB *keeps forcing products into her hands.*)

BOB: We're *free*, right? This is *freedom*. Here...here's
a toaster. It's yours. All yours. Here, Maura. Here's
another one. Here you go. Dan? Here, Dan. Danny?
Dan? I got a nice little product for you, Danny...a nice
little *consumer* item...right here for you, boy. Whoops,
it looks like Dan's a little spent. Oh, here, Maura, look
here at this one. This looks like an entertaining little
consumer *product*. No? What's the matter, folks? Not so
entertaining, this *consumer* item? Oh, gosh. Oh my. This
is just terrible. I don't think they find it entertaining,
Chip. Here I am, offering them a perfectly entertaining
product, virtually *free*, and I'm getting no response at all.

CHIP: Uh...that could be a problem, Bob.

BOB: Oh, yeah? How's that, Chip?

CHIP: Well, Bob, we're sort of in the entertainment
business.

BOB: Are we, Chip? Is *that* what doing here? We're in
the entertainment *business*, are we?

CHIP: Last time I checked, Bob. Yes. Why? Did
you...want to be doing something *else*, Bob?

BOB: Hmm. Something *else*. I wonder what that would
be?

MAURA: *(In shock, staring out)* How can you do this?
Don't you have any feelings?

BOB: What the hell are you talking about, Maura?

MAURA: Feelings. Emotions. Doesn't this bother you?
What you're doing to us?

BOB: Maura, Maura. I'm just a guy on T V. I'm just a
character in a *T V* show...that isn't *real*. I'm a figment of
your imagination. How could I have feelings, Maura?
Now, *opinions* I've got. Sentiments. Reactions. Problem
is, they change according to what's popular at the
moment. They are *programmed in*, understand? They

have been put there, *Maura*. Planted. Implanted.
Designed. Installed. They come from the *factory*. Does
this sound *familiar*? They are not mine. They are like
some kind of software installed in my brain. They tell
me what to do, what to think, how to feel, what to
believe, on a moment by moment basis. Other people's
ideas. Other people's thoughts. Emotional triggers.
Manufactured desires. I have no connection to myself,
Maura. I have no *center*, no ground to stand on. I am on
a plastic gerbil wheel. I am juggling plates. I am trying,
desperately, to follow different sets of contradictory
instructions. I cannot keep this up much longer, or I
will go completely fucking insane, and become a robot,
a zombie, a vegetable...a vegetable following orders,
Maura. And I do not want to be a vegetable that follows
orders, Maura. I want to be a *living* being. Don't you
want to be a living being? Alive. Sentient. Present.
Awake. Please say that you understand this, Maura.
Please, please, tell me that you understand this.

(Pause. Everyone frozen in place for a moment, MAURA
staring straight out, in shock, completely shattered.)

MAURA: Oh God... He's dead.

BOB: Maura?! Hello?!

CHIP: Uh, I think Maura is trying to *say* something, Bob.

BOB: Oh? Is she? Alright. What is it? What is it that you
wanted to *say*, Maura?

MAURA: He's dead.

BOB: Who's dead? Who is dead, Maura?

MAURA: He is. He's dead. Dan is dead.

BOB: Oh, *Dan. Dan* is dead. Yes, of course he is.
Along with everything he represents. It's all dead.
It's been dead for years.

MAURA: I don't understand.

BOB: Yes. You do.

MAURA: Dan's my husband...we're a family.

BOB: A family? How quaint. Did you see that on T V?

MAURA: We had a son...

BOB: Yes, but he's *dead*. Isn't he, Maura, this *son*, you had?

MAURA: Yes. He died.

BOB: Yes. He did. He died...and he's gone. And he's never coming back.

MAURA: Never?

BOB: Never.

MAURA: Oh God...God...all I wanted...was to come to California....

BOB: And now you're here.

MAURA: And be on the show...

BOB: And now you are.

MAURA: And play...the game...the normal game... that everybody plays.

BOB: This *is* the normal game, Maura, that everybody plays. This *is* the game. And you're the only one left, honey. And you know what *that* means!

(Canned applause, bells, lighting effects, etc)

CHIP: It looks like you're our *winner*, Maura! Congratulations! How does it feel?!

MAURA: Oh God. I'm dying.

BOB: No, you're winning.

MAURA: It's dead...I'm dead.

BOB: No. *Dan* is dead.

MAURA: And I'm alive?

BOB: Well, I wouldn't go that far.

MAURA: Wait...what's happening? Is this still the show?

BOB: Of course it is. It's all the show.

MAURA: I don't understand. I don't know where we are. *(Pause)* What *is* this? Who *are* you?

BOB: Christ, I thought you'd never ask. Who does it seem like I am to you, Maura?

MAURA: You're Bob. You're...the *host*.

BOB: The *host*? Hmm.

(Pause)

MAURA: You're Bob. Big Bob. This is the Big Bob Show.

(Pause)

MAURA: You're *not* Big Bob. You're not the real host.

BOB: No? Are you sure?

MAURA: Oh God, what is this?

BOB: Gee, I don't know. From the way you describe it, kind of sounds like one of those Greek tragedies to me. Doesn't it sound like that to you, Chip?

CHIP: As a matter of fact it *does*, Bob, now that you mention it...it sounds just *like* one of those ancient Greek tragedies.

BOB: Like the kind where everybody *dies* in the end, Chip? Where the gods just smash their little worlds to pieces...their families...their kingdoms...their little empires...all their little dreams that they take for real...and they tear their eyes out and cut their own throats after realizing how blind and arrogant they had been? *(Crosses upstage, leaving MAURA alone)*

CHIP: Yes, well, you know those wacky *Greeks*, Bob.

MAURA: *(Talking to herself, facing out)* This is the Big Bob Show. That's what this is. We're on the show. This is the show. Dan is my husband. We're in California.

BOB: How nice for you.

MAURA: This *is* real. You *are* the host. This *is* the game. It's just a game...a game we're playing...on television. I know who I am. I know what is real. I know what is true. You're lying. You're evil. I'm not going to talk to you. *(She addresses the imaginary camera again.)* Hi, this is Maura...Maura Brown...from Johnstown, somewhere. I'm talking to you...sitting there watching...at home... watching. This is real. It's not supposed to be. I don't know what happened. Something went wrong. Bob isn't Bob. Bob's an impostor. And Vera's a man. They killed my Dan. And we're all here...we're all in Los Angeles somewhere, I think. This is America. Is this America? We're not supposed to die. Not like this. We're supposed to win. If we do what they tell us... we're supposed to win things. Things on T V. Did we do something wrong? What did we do? We don't deserve this. We're not monsters. We're not like the Germans or the Russians or the Romans. We're not bad people. We're not...evil. We're good. Good people. We're the good people. We love...our families...and freedom, and I...don't know why this happened. We did what they told us. We followed...

BOB: *(Softly, from upstage)* What, Maura? What did you follow?

MAURA: We did what you told us. We did what they told us.

BOB: What did they tell you?

MAURA: Everything. I don't know. Stop it. Listen. Don't believe them. They lie. They're liars. They call you on the phone. They send a little card...an invitation...to come to Burbank, California...to be on T V...to play the

game. It looks so pretty. And there's a picture of Bob...
smiling, and his hand...is reaching out to you...but it's
all a bunch of lies...and you can't tell which...are the
lies...and the truth. And once you believe it...then
you're in it...then it starts...and once it starts...it never
stops...and you never win...and it just keeps changing...
and there's nothing underneath...and there's nothing
inside...and you can't even fight it. It's just too big.
It's everything...everywhere...replacing everything.
It's coming. Can't you see it? It's already here. Don't
believe in it. Don't be like us. We thought we knew.
We thought we were so... Look at us. Look at us.
What have we become? I'm sorry. I'm sorry... This
doesn't make sense. I don't know what I'm saying.
I don't know who I am. Am I someone on T V? Am
I a T V person? Am I a real person? *(Pause)* I'm Maura
Brown. *(Pause)* I'm Maura Brown. *(Pause)* I'm Maura
Brown. I live here. Help me.

*(Blackout. After a moment, theme music variation rises
slowly and lights fade back up slowly on the empty stage.)*

CHIP: Well... that's going to do it for us here tonight,
folks. Folks at home, thanks for tuning in! Folks in the
studio, let's give the Browns a hand! Dan and Maura!

(Canned applause)

CHIP: Dan and Maura Brown!

(Canned applause)

CHIP: So then, until next time, this is Chip Devlin,
saying...good night, Bob...and, uh... *(Clears throat)*
...good night, America.

(Blackout)

END OF PLAY